KFK KINGFISHER KNOWLE

D1386324

NATURAL DISASTERS

Previous page: St Mark's Square in Venice, Italy, lies under 1.5m of water after a violent storm lashed the city in 1996.

This page: A volcanologist collects samples of lava from Mount Etna, Sicily, Italy. In the background, a fountain of lava erupts from the volcano, which is the most active in Europe.

NATURAL DISASTERS

Andrew Langley

Foreword by
Bill McGuire

KINGFISHER

First published 2006 by Kingfisher

This edition published 2008 by Kingfisher
an imprint of Macmillan Children's Books
a division of Macmillan Publishers Limited
The Macmillan Building, 4 Crinan Street, London N1 9XW
Basingstoke and Oxford
Associated companies throughout the world
www.panmacmillan.com

ISBN 978-0-7534-1366-1

Copyright © Macmillan Children's Books 2006

9 8 7 6 5 4 3 2 1
1TR/0808/TWP/MA(MA)/130/GRYMA/F

A CIP catalogue record for this book is available from the British Library.

Printed in Singapore

NOTE TO READERS

The website addresses listed in this book are correct at the
time of going to print. However, due to the ever-changing
nature of the internet, website addresses and content can
change. Websites can contain links that are unsuitable for
children. The publisher cannot be held responsible for
changes in website addresses or content, or for information
obtained through third-party websites. We strongly advise
that internet searches should be supervised by an adult.

GO FURTHER...
INFORMATION PANEL KEY:

 websites and
further reading

 career paths

 places to visit

Contents

▼ A violent earthquake in 1999, which
killed more than 2,400 people, caused
this building to collapse in Taipei, Taiwan.

Foreword

Our wonderful planet earth provides for all our needs. It gives us water to drink, fertile soils in which to plant our crops, wind to fly a kite, and snow to let you race down a mountainside on a snowboard. But it also has a dark side. The gentle rains can become a torrential downpour that feeds raging flood waters, the fertile soils on the flanks of volcanoes can be buried beneath rivers of molten lava, while the whispering breezes and snow flurries can become devastating storms and freezing blizzards.

Studying natural hazards such as storms, earthquakes and volcanic eruptions can be dangerous, but also very rewarding. On a dark September night nearly ten years ago, I was working as a volcanologist on the beautiful Caribbean island of Montserrat. I was woken by a growing rumble that sounded exactly like a jumbo jet taking off. The noise wasn't an aircraft, but Montserrat's Soufriere Hills volcano blasting into life. Within seconds, a huge cloud of ash had surged into the sky and small lumps of rock clattered onto roofs and cars. This was really scary. We didn't know how big the eruption was going to be, or even if we would survive, but we had to get to work. Nearly a thousand people were still living in the volcano's immediate vicinity and they needed help to leave the danger zone. With a couple of colleagues, I drove towards the volcano to find out what was going on and to offer assistance to terrified men, women and children. Fortunately, the eruption lasted only 45 minutes and no-one was killed or injured, but its memory will always be with me. If the explosion had been much larger, neither I nor my colleagues would be here to tell the tale. When the ash had cleared and the morning dawned bright and sunny, it felt good to be alive and to have helped to evacuate so many people.

Natural hazards will always be with us and people will always be needed to try to understand the processes that cause them, to monitor them and predict when they might next happen, and to try to prevent them leading to great disasters such as the Indian ocean tsunami or the recent devastation of New Orleans by Hurricane Katrina. This book is called *Natural Disasters* and it provides a fantastic introduction to the science of natural hazards, their effects, and how we might cope with the worst they can throw at us. Hopefully, it will inspire you to learn more about these awe-inspiring but dangerous phenomena and join the ranks of our future volcanologists, earthquake scientists or storm chasers. There will always be more that we need to know, and as the population of our planet increases and global warming begins to take hold, increasing numbers of hazards and even bigger disasters mean that we will need all the help we can get. Good luck!

Professor Bill McGuire
Benfield Professor and Director, Benfield Hazard Research Centre

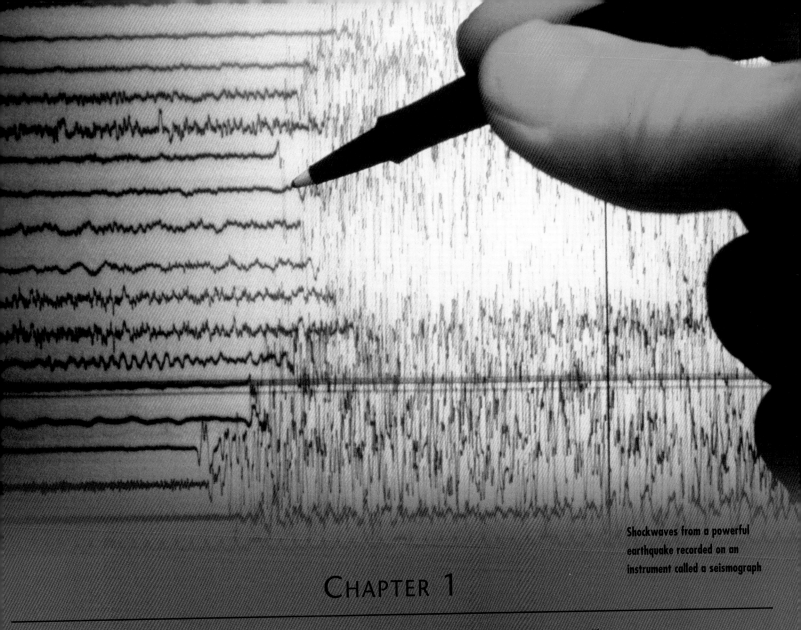

Shockwaves from a powerful
earthquake recorded on an
instrument called a seismograph

CHAPTER 1

The restless earth

Every year there are about one million earthquakes throughout the world. Most are minor tremors, taking place far below the ground. But occasionally a much more powerful earthquake strikes, unleashing the equivalent energy of several nuclear bombs. When major earthquakes happen near densely populated areas, they can cause catastrophic damage. They shake and split the surface of the earth, destroying whole cities, killing thousands of people and leaving many more homeless. Earthquakes can also trigger massive waves called tsunamis. These build up into walls of water that flood low-lying coastlines, spreading the devastation over an even wider area. It has been estimated that, during the last century, earthquakes resulted in the deaths of more than two million people across the planet.

Moving ground

The ground beneath our feet feels solid and still. In fact, it is moving all the time. The outer layer of the earth is broken up into huge plates, like the pieces of a gigantic jigsaw puzzle. These plates are constantly in motion, very slowly being pushed together or pulled apart. When they slide and clash against each other, the plates can produce shockwaves, which we experience as earthquakes.

▲ The shockwaves from an earthquake cause buildings to collapse with devastating results. These cars were crushed like matchboxes during an earthquake at Northridge, near Los Angeles, California, USA, in 1994. The quake killed 57 people.

Floating world

Humans live on the surface of the earth's outer covering, which is called the lithosphere. This rocky layer, which can be up to 500km thick in places, includes the crust and the top part of the mantle. The lithosphere consists of seven major tectonic plates and several smaller ones. Below the lithosphere is the asthenosphere, a layer made up of molten and liquid material. Scientists believe that the plates float on this layer, shifting by as much as 5cm in a year. This may not seem very much, but it is enough to have far-reaching consequences, including earthquakes.

Seismic waves

Some plates move apart, allowing molten rock to well up through the gap from below and solidify. Others move together. This head-on clash of plates can have several results. The plates may crumple up into mountain ranges over millions of years, or grind alongside each other. The constant squeezing and stretching of the plate edges builds up stresses in the rock, which eventually ruptures and causes an earthquake. The point directly above the earthquake is called the epicentre. The energy released travels outwards in a series of seismic waves, or vibrations. These grow weaker as they travel further from the epicentre, but may still be felt as far as 1,600km away.

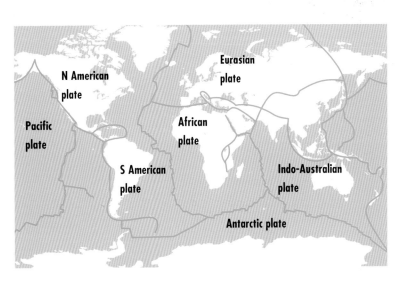

▲ The surface of the earth is made up of seven main tectonic plates. Their movement is the cause of many of the planet's major processes, such as the drifting of the continents, earthquakes and volcanoes.

▼ Rescue workers search for survivors in the ruins of a building after an earthquake in Taipei, Taiwan, in September 1999. The earthquake shook the whole island, destroying over 10,000 homes and killing more than 2,000 people.

Danger zones

Almost all major earthquakes occur at the edges of the plates, where one meets another. The world's main danger zone is at the border of the Pacific plate, a crack that runs around the rim of the Pacific ocean. Over half of all earthquakes occur along this line, as well as many volcanic eruptions. The other big earthquake area is the belt running from the Mediterranean eastwards to China, where the Eurasian plate meets the African and Indo-Australian plates.

Earthquake!

A great scar in the earth's crust runs for over 960km along the coast of California, USA. This is the San Andreas Fault, where the Pacific plate grinds slowly along the North American plate. On 18 April 1906, a sudden break in the rock shifted the ground 6m. This triggered an earthquake that rocked San Francisco, and started fires which destroyed the city centre. Over 2,500 people were killed. In 1989, another major earthquake hit the area.

▲ The valley-like crack of the San Andreas Fault, California, USA, marks the boundary between two plates. During an earthquake, the ground on either side of the fault can move by up to 12m in a few seconds.

Earthquake-resistant buildings

Collapsing houses, fires and floods cause most of the deaths during earthquakes. Engineers have tried to develop ways of building houses that can survive seismic shocks in areas frequently hit by earth tremors. Light, two-storey houses with timber frames suffer less damage than old-fashioned stone or brick ones. Some buildings are now constructed from extra-strong concrete with an outer wall of steel to make them less likely to collapse.

▼ The epicentre of the San Francisco earthquake of 1906 was very close to the city itself. Fires caused by broken gas mains and arson burned much of the city to the ground after the quake.

Vulnerable Japan

Japan lies at the meeting point of three tectonic plates – the Eurasian, the Pacific and the Philippine. As a result, the country suffers more earthquakes than any other part of the world. Nearly ten per cent of all seismic shocks happen in the region. In 1923, over 150,000 people were killed by an earthquake. A more recent quake flattened the city of Kobe in 1995, killing 5,400 people.

South Asia earthquake 2005

Another danger area is the Himalayan mountains in south Asia, where one tectonic plate pushes into another. A major earthquake hit northern Pakistan on 8 October 2005. The tremors twisted the landscape and wrecked buildings over a span of 400km, and shook parts of Afghanistan and India. Early figures showed that over 70,000 people died in the disaster.

▲ Nearly 250,000 people were made homeless by the earthquake which hit Kobe, Japan, in January 1995. Despite near-freezing temperatures, many preferred to sleep outdoors for fear of aftershocks.

▼ In 1989, San Francisco suffered its most severe earthquake since the 1906 quake. More than 3,500 people were injured and there were 66 deaths. At the time, it was the most expensive natural disaster in US history.

Tsunami terror

A stone dropping into a pond sends out a widening circle of ripples. In the same way, an earthquake under the sea creates a series of waves that can travel many thousands of kilometres. These monster waves, called tsunamis, can have a terrible impact when they crash ashore. Tsunami means 'harbour wave' in Japanese. The term was originally used by fishermen who returned to port to discover devastation in the surrounding area.

▶ Most tsunamis are caused by undersea earthquakes that convulse the ocean floor. Underwater volcanoes and landslides can also trigger tsunamis.

▶ In open water, the fast-moving tsunami wave may reach only 1m in height, but its immense energy extends down to the seabed.

▶ As it nears the shore, the wave slows down and rapidly becomes steeper and taller. A series of tsunami waves may follow the leading one.

Earthquakes at sea

Most major tsunamis are caused by earthquakes on fault lines under, or near, the ocean. A sudden upward or downward shift in the ocean floor acts like a giant paddle, pushing away an immense volume of the surrounding water. A series of waves, sometimes hundreds of kilometres apart, radiates out through the sea. In open water, the crest of the wave is never very high above the surface. People on boats may not even notice that a tsunami has passed under them.

▲ Fire raged through Lisbon for five days after it was struck by an earthquake and a series of tsunamis in 1755. Out of a population of 275,000, almost 90,000 people were killed.

Double disaster

Earthquakes and tsunamis are terrifying prospects on their own. But sometimes they strike together. On 1 November 1755, Lisbon, the capital of Portugal, suffered a major earthquake. Buildings fell, instantly burying hundreds of people. However, many people fled to the harbour, believing that they would be safe there. Soon afterwards tsunamis raced in from the Atlantic, flooding the dock area and sweeping people to their deaths.

Hitting the coast

A tsunami can travel across the ocean at speeds of up to 800km/h, which is as fast as a jet aircraft. As it nears the coastline, the tsunami slows down, but rapidly rears up to a great height. By the time it reaches the shore, the wave can reach a height of 30m or more. The force of a tsunami can reduce buildings to rubble and can carry boats and boulders several kilometres inland.

▼ After travelling thousands of kilometres across the ocean, the destructive energy of a tsunami is released as it crashes ashore. The immense weight of water can destroy everything in its path.

▲ Animals often display unusual behaviour before an earthquake or tsunami. These Chinese government posters show people what to look out for before such an event.

The Indian ocean tsunami

The tsunami of 26 December 2004 was one of the deadliest natural disasters in recorded history. It began on the sea floor of the Indian ocean, to the northwest of Sumatra. Two tectonic plates meet at this point, and one slides under the other. The huge stresses that build up at this faultline were suddenly released, triggering an extremely powerful earthquake. As a result, the sea floor was rapidly thrust upward by 20m, displacing billions of tonnes of seawater.

▲ People flee in terror as the first tsunami crashes ashore in the Andaman islands on 26 December 2004. The photographer who took this picture escaped unhurt, then watched two more giant waves from higher ground.

▼ Soldiers carry away a damaged fishing boat from a beach in southern India battered by the tsunami. In India alone, over 350,000 people were made homeless.

Panic on the beaches

Waves hurtled across the ocean in every direction. Within 30 minutes, they had reached the coast of Sumatra to the east, crashing inland at a height of 20m. The tsunami also raced further north, towards the coast of Thailand. More waves, thousands of kilometres to the west, devastated the southern tip of Sri Lanka.

▲ Many countries (red) around the rim of the Indian ocean were directly affected by the 2004 tsunami. The waves radiated from the epicentre, off the coast of Sumatra, Indonesia, even reaching the coast of East Africa.

Future recovery

Over 300,000 people died in the Indian ocean tsunami and many bodies were never recovered. Apart from the terrible loss of life, the disaster robbed the survivors of homes, possessions, food, clean water supplies and vital farmland. A worldwide relief fund raised several hundred million pounds but recovery will take many years.

Warning systems

When the tsunami struck, the Indian ocean had no warning system, unlike in the Pacific ocean. Here, a network of observatories monitors tide levels and indications of earthquakes. Information is sent to the Tsunami Warning Center in Honolulu, USA, and people can be alerted well in advance of any impending tsunami.

▲ Many coastal communities were completely destroyed by the Indian ocean tsunami. Six months after the disaster, these Sri Lankan villagers were still clearing the rubble from their homes.

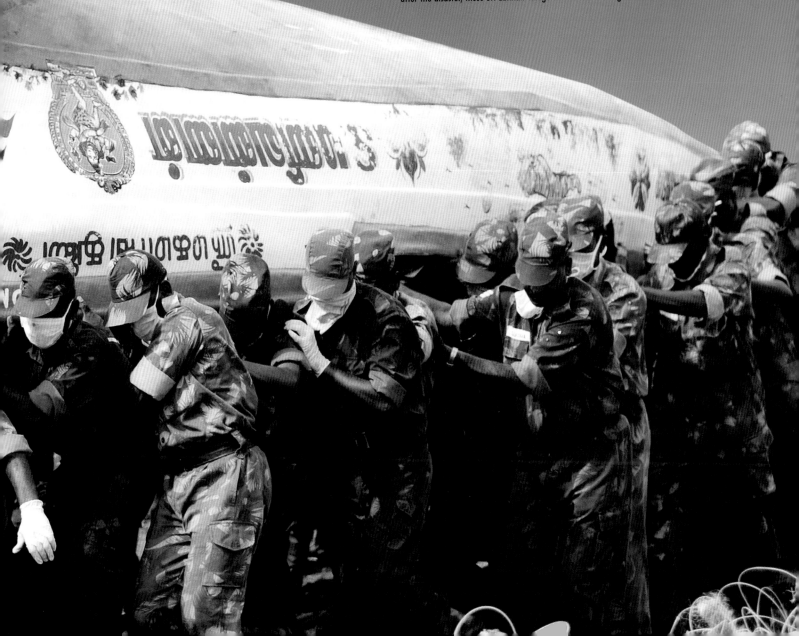

Understanding quakes

Ancient legends explained earthquakes as the work of the gods. The Fijians of the Pacific believed tremors were caused by the movements of the god who carried the world on his shoulders. An ancient Japanese myth told of a giant catfish which lay underground, creating earthquakes with its thrashing tail. Today, scientists have a much greater understanding of seismic activity. Despite modern technology, however, earthquakes are still notoriously difficult to predict with any accuracy.

▲ A Chinese scientist designed this instrument in about 32CE. Shockwaves from an earthquake move a pendulum inside. This opens the jaws of the dragon facing the direction of the earthquake. A ball then falls into the mouth of the toad below.

▼ A seismologist at Taiwan's Central Weather Bureau, Taipei, examines seismic waves produced by two earthquakes that struck Taiwan on 14 June 2001. Both measured more than six on the Richter scale but, fortunately, there were no casualties.

Measuring equipment

One key instrument for earthquake detection is the seismograph, which can record underground movements. The first practical seismograph was developed by John Milne in 1880. A pen attached to a weight on a pendulum was suspended from a frame fixed firmly to the ground. Any seismic waves were recorded on a roll of paper. Modern seismographs use electronic motion sensors, amplifiers and recording equipment.

Waves

Earthquakes generate three different kinds of waves. A Primary Wave travels fastest, and can move through solid rock, as well as water and even molten magma in a volcano. It pushes and pulls the rock, causing vertical movement. A Secondary Wave distorts the rock, shearing it from side to side and making the ground move vertically and horizontally. A Surface Wave is like the ripple on a pond. It is produced by the first two kinds of wave when they are very near to the earth's surface.

The Richter scale

In 1935, Charles Richter devised a way of measuring an earthquake based on the energy released. A minor tremor ranks as two or less on the Richter scale. An earthquake over five, however, is strong enough to cause structural damage to buildings. The most violent quakes generally measure eight or greater. The Indian ocean tsunami, in 2004, was triggered by a quake rated at 9.1 – one of the most powerful ever recorded. Another system – the Mercalli scale – is used to measure effects on the surface such as chimneys falling down (VII), rail tracks bending (X) and total destruction (XII).

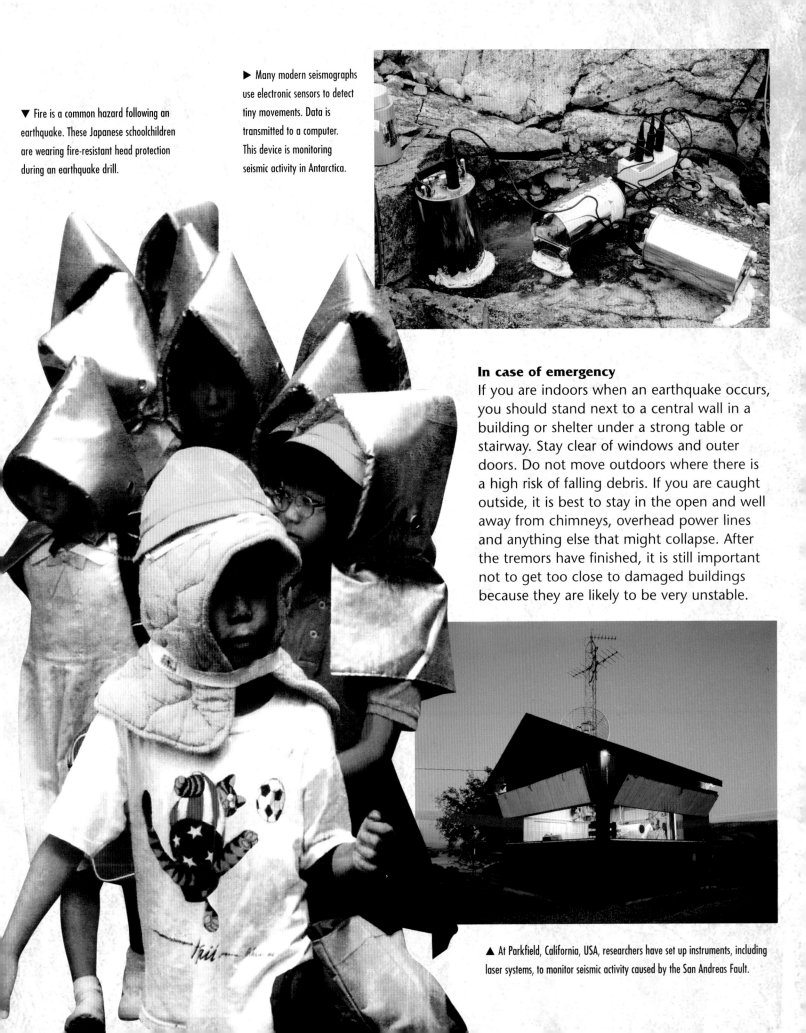

▼ Fire is a common hazard following an earthquake. These Japanese schoolchildren are wearing fire-resistant head protection during an earthquake drill.

▶ Many modern seismographs use electronic sensors to detect tiny movements. Data is transmitted to a computer. This device is monitoring seismic activity in Antarctica.

In case of emergency

If you are indoors when an earthquake occurs, you should stand next to a central wall in a building or shelter under a strong table or stairway. Stay clear of windows and outer doors. Do not move outdoors where there is a high risk of falling debris. If you are caught outside, it is best to stay in the open and well away from chimneys, overhead power lines and anything else that might collapse. After the tremors have finished, it is still important not to get too close to damaged buildings because they are likely to be very unstable.

▲ At Parkfield, California, USA, researchers have set up instruments, including laser systems, to monitor seismic activity caused by the San Andreas Fault.

SUMMARY OF CHAPTER 1: THE RESTLESS EARTH

Under the earth

The outer layer of the earth consists of vast drifting slabs of rock, called tectonic plates. These float on the mantle – a layer of molten and liquid rock deep underground. The plates are in constant motion, some drifting apart, some colliding, and others rubbing and squeezing against each other. The boundary between two plates is called a fault. Sometimes, the plates 'stick' and stress builds up in the rock at the plate edges. Eventually this ruptures and creates violent tremors – an earthquake. The energy from the rupture moves outwards in a series of vibrations called seismic waves. The point on the surface directly above the source of the seismic waves is called the epicentre. The waves grow weaker as they travel away

Extensive damage caused by an earthquake in Northridge, near Los Angeles, California, USA

from the epicentre. The areas in the world that are most at risk from earthquakes lie near the faultlines. When an earthquake occurs on a faultline under the sea, it can trigger a tsunami. A sudden upward or downward shift in the ocean floor shifts huge volumes of water that form tsunamis. The waves can travel across the ocean at speeds of up to 800km/h. Out at sea, the waves can pass unnoticed under a boat. When they reach the coast, however, they slow down and rear up in the shallower water. As it crashes ashore, a tsunami can reach up to 30m in height. The force of the impact can destroy everything in its path and cause severe flooding.

Measuring earthquakes

Although earthquakes are difficult to predict accurately, scientists constantly monitor earthquake activity worldwide. They use instruments such as the seismograph for detecting movement under the ground. The size, or 'magnitude', of an earthquake is measured on the Richter scale, based on the energy released by the quake, or the Mercalli scale, which charts the damage that results.

Go further...

Track earthquakes throughout the world at: www.earthquakes.com

Find more about earthquakes at: www.earthquake.usgs.gov

Learn more about the 2004 Indian ocean tsunami at: www.pbs.org/wgbh/nova/tsunami/

Earthquakes in Human History by Jelle Zeilinga de Boer and Donald Sanders (Princeton, 2004)

Tsunami by Ann Morris and Heidi Larson (Lerner Publications, 2005)

Eyewitness: Volcanoes and Earthquakes by Susanna Van Rose (Dorling Kindersley, 2004)

Geomagnetist
Measures the earth's magnetic field and explores the planet's orgins.

Geophysicist
Studies the physics of the earth, and the processes that take place inside our planet and on the surface.

Paleomagnetist
Interprets fossil evidence in rocks and sediments from continents and oceans to record spreading of sea floor and continental drift.

Seismologist
Monitors earthquakes and the shockwaves they produce in the earth.

See exciting earthquake features in the Earth Galleries of the Natural History Museum: Cromwell Road, London SW7 5BD, UK Telephone: +44 (0) 20 7942 5000 www.nhm.ac.uk/visit-us/galleries

Interact with the quake exhibits at The Exploratorium Learning Studio: 3601 Lyon Street, San Francisco, California, USA www.exploratorium.edu/

Discover more about the workings of the planet at The Sedgwick Museum of Earth Sciences: University of Cambridge, Downing Street, Cambridge CB2 3EQ, UK Telephone: +44 (0)1223 333456 www.sedgwickmuseum.org

A spectacular flow
of lava pours
from a volcano

CHAPTER 2

Volcanoes

A volcanic eruption is one of the natural world's most awe-inspiring events. Vast clouds of suffocating ash, rivers of scalding lava, lumps of molten rock hurled through the air, and catastrophic explosions are some of the deadly results of eruptions. Volcanoes that erupt regularly are called active volcanoes and most lie near the earth's weak spots at the tectonic plate boundaries. The name volcano comes from Vulcan, the ancient Roman god of fire (in the past, people believed that angry gods lived inside them). Living in the shadow of a volcano can be extremely dangerous. However, many people do, because volcanic soil is very fertile. Volcanic eruptions have caused some of the worst disasters in history. It has been estimated that over one million people have died as a result of volcanic activity in the past 2,000 years. Some historians believe that volcanoes have even been responsible for destroying several ancient civilizations.

Eruption!

Volcanoes are openings in the earth. During an eruption, molten rock, or magma, makes its way upwards from deep inside the mantle, as far as 160km below the earth's surface. The magma, mixed with gases, bursts through the crust and flows out as lava. Rock, ash, steam and hot gases may erupt with it. The lava eventually cools and solidifies around the vent, sometimes forming a volcano's familiar cone shape.

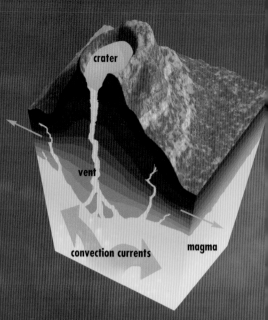

▶ A volcano erupts when magma inside the magma chamber below the volcano builds up enough pressure to rise through the vent. Currents called convection currents, together with the movement of tectonic plates, can produce cracks in the crust where a volcano forms.

crater

vent

convection currents

magma

Cracks and hot spots

The majority of volcanoes occur along the cracks in the lithosphere which mark the edges of the world's tectonic plates. These are the weakest spots in the earth's surface. There are, however, some eruptions in the middle of plates (such as Kilauea, Hawaii, USA, which is a long way from the edge). The places where these occur are called hot spots. Scientists believe that they are made by thin plumes of very hot magma which rise up and punch holes in the plate.

Asia

Aleutian islands

North America

Pacific ocean

South America

New Zealand

▲ Most volcanoes (red dots) are found on the boundaries between the earth's tectonic plates (grey lines). Around the Pacific ocean is the Ring of Fire – a great arc that stretches from New Zealand, along the eastern edge of Asia, north across the Aleutian islands of Alaska, and south along the coast of North and South America. Almost 75 per cent of the world's volcanoes are found here. It is located at the edges of the Pacific plate and other tectonic plates.

Types of volcano

Volcanoes come in different shapes depending on the type of eruption. Shield volcanoes have shallow, sloping sides and are formed by very hot, runny lava that spreads over a wide area. Cone-shaped volcanoes result from thick layers of volcanic ash and cinders that erupt from a central crater. More explosive eruptions create broad craters called calderas.

Building and destroying

A volcano, like other violent natural forces, can transform a landscape beyond recognition. It can create land with its lava, even giving birth to new islands out at sea. It can form vast underground tunnels, as well as dramatic shapes where the lava cools, including ledges, pillars and domes. And, of course, a volcano can also obliterate a landscape, smothering it with red-hot rock and ash, or blasting it with superheated gases.

► The island of Surtsey, southwest of Iceland, rose out of the sea in a single day in 1963. It was created by a volcanic eruption of lava on the ocean bed. Within two years, Surtsey was 180m high and 2.4km across.

▼ Liquified rock, or magma, emerges from a volcano's crater as lava. The steep sides of this volcano in Montserrat have been formed by thick lava cooling and hardening before it had a chance to spread very far.

▼ A red-hot river of lava engulfs a house on Heimaey, an island off Iceland, during the long eruption of 1973. Ash and lava flows forced people to abandon the island's only town.

Buried by lava

In June 1783, a series of earthquakes shook Mount Skaptar in Iceland, a country that has over 180 volcanoes. A fissure, or crack, opened up in the Laki volcano on the side of the mountain. Out of it poured a flood of lava, which kept flowing for five long months. By the end of the year, lava covered a large part of the country, burying many villages and fields. The lava flows were so hot that they melted nearby glaciers, causing extensive flooding across the country.

◀ The bodies of people buried by ash from Vesuvius decomposed, leaving hollow casts. When these were filled with plaster 1,800 years later, the victims were revealed.

▶ Pahoehoe lava can easily outrun a person. This runny lava solidifies into smooth, unusual shapes and is sometimes called lava sculpture.

▶ Thicker lava, which moves more slowly and cools with a thick skin, is called 'aa' lava. This breaks up to form jagged and twisted rock.

▶ Very hot, fluid lava flows from Kilauea volcano on the island of Hawaii, USA. When the lava reaches the sea, it cools to form solid rock.

From liquid to rock

When lava leaves the volcano's vent it is a liquid that can reach temperatures as high as 1,200°C. Lava can flow many kilometres before it starts to cool. Eventually, it hardens into rock. But its final shape and texture can vary, depending on how hot it was when it emerged from the volcano.

Poison from the sky

Lava scorches and buries everything in its path. Volcanoes can also produce other deadly substances. The Laki eruption released vast clouds of poisonous fumes from the vent that hung over the landscape for several months. This killed off sheep, cattle and crops, and caused a famine that eventually wiped out one-fifth of the population of Iceland.

Roman tragedy

In August 79CE, Mount Vesuvius in Italy erupted. Pyroclastic flows, made up of hot gas, ash and molten rock, exploded out of the volcano. People in the nearby town of Pompeii suffocated or burned to death. On the other side of the mountain, the town of Herculaneum disappeared under a deluge of mud and ash.

▼ Following the eruption in June 1991 of Mount Pinatubo in the Philippines, nearby towns and villages were covered in a thick carpet of ash.

Exploding volcanoes

A volcano generates a staggering amount of energy. In many eruptions, this energy is released as the lava and gases flow out. But suppose the energy cannot escape. What if the lava moves so slowly that it blocks the vent? The intense heat and the gas pressure build up inside the volcano until there is only one possible result – the volcano is blown apart in a gigantic explosion.

▲ Islanders watch as clouds of ash emerge from Mount Pelée in May 1902. Despite this warning sign that the volcano was about to erupt, most people did not evacuate.

▲ When Mount Pelée erupted, fire and the force of the explosion reduced the town of St Pierre to rubble. One of the two survivors was a prisoner in the town's jail.

▼ Trees flattened by the blast from Mount St Helens in 1980 cover the surface of nearby Spirit lake. It has been estimated that the eruption released the equivalent amount of energy to 27,000 Hiroshima-sized atomic bombs.

Caribbean tragedy

Early in 1902, Mount Pelée, on the Caribbean island of Martinique, began to grow. The volcano, which lay at the top of the mountain, had been plugged by a build-up of lava. Over the next few months, this pushed itself skywards in a rocky spike, until it was 600m above the crater. On 8 May, the mountain exploded and expelled a searing blast of superheated gas. In only three minutes, the nearby town of St Pierre was completely destroyed. Out of the population of 28,000 people, there were only two survivors.

Deadly cloud

The cloud of gas, ash and rock fragments from the Mount Pelée eruption travelled at 33m per second, leaving no time for escape. After burning the town, it rolled out to sea and set fire to ships. One eyewitness described how 'the side of the volcano was ripped out, and there hurled straight towards us a solid wall of flame… it was like a hurricane of fire'. Scientists now describe this kind of extreme volcanic eruption as a pyroclastic flow. The 1902 disaster was widely reported across the world and made people much more aware of the dangers posed by active volcanoes.

Volcano watch

Today, scientists closely monitor the behaviour of active volcanoes. Satellite technology, such as the Global Positioning System (GPS), is used to make frequent measurements of a mountain's shape in order to detect any changes. When magma rises to the surface, it may cause the top of the mountain to bulge – a sign that a volcano might erupt. In 1980, scientists identified such a bulge on Mount St Helens, Washington state, USA. The area was cleared, and two months later the volcano exploded. Although 57 people died, the death toll would have been much higher without the early warning.

▲ Mount St Helens had been dormant for over a century when it exploded with catastrophic results in May 1980. The nine hour eruption destroyed all living things within an area of about 180km² and volcanic ash rained down on 11 US States. Glaciers on the mountain melted and triggered lahars, or volcanic mudslides. The top of the mountain disintegrated, reducing its height from 2,950m to 2,550m and forming a 1.5km-wide horseshoe-shaped crater. Mount St Helens is still active over 25 years later.

After the eruption

A volcanic eruption can bring devastation to the surrounding area within a few minutes. But volcanoes can also have an impact on distant places and may even change weather patterns around the world. When a volcano exploded on the tiny Indonesian island of Krakatoa on 27 August 1883, it could be heard as far as southern Australia, over 3,200km away. The explosion destroyed most of the island, but worse was to follow. The volcano collapsed into the sea triggering tsunamis, which could be felt as far away as South Africa.

▲ This historical print shows an ash cloud emerging from Krakatoa during the early stages of its eruption in 1883. The main island was destroyed in the explosion, but today there are four small islands covered in forest on the site.

Blotting out the sun

The explosion of Krakatoa also blasted a huge cloud of ash over 80km into the sky. It was so dense that the region around the island suffered two days of total darkness. Crops and vegetation in Java and Sumatra were destroyed by the ash falls. Air currents carried the cloud several times around the earth, and the light reflecting on the countless dust particles created a series of brilliantly coloured sunsets in Europe and North America.

◀ A satellite picture taken soon after the eruption of Mount Pinatubo in the Philippines in 1991 highlights the spreading airborne particles, or aerosols, that were released high into the atmosphere.

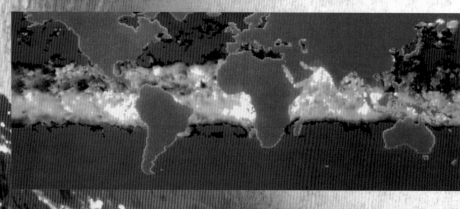

◀ Eight weeks later, the cloud of aerosols had spread across the planet. As well as causing very red sunrises and sunsets, the cloud reflected some of the sun's heat back into space, lowering the earth's temperature by about 0.5°C.

A flood of mud

As well as tsunamis, there are other dangers when volcanoes and water meet. If there is heavy rainfall following an eruption, the combination of ash and rain can create a river of mud, which races down the mountainside, burying everything below. In 1919, a mudflow at the Kelut volcano in Java left 5,500 people dead. Another threat comes from the lakes that sometimes form in volcanic craters. If a lake fractures in an eruption, its contents can produce a massive mudflow.

End of a civilization

Major eruptions can sometimes change the course of history. Over 3,000 years ago, the Minoan people of Crete were the most powerful in the Mediterranean. In 1650BCE, however, Thera volcano on the island of Santorini, 70km to the south of Crete, was shattered by a powerful eruption. This set off a tsunami, possibly 30m in height, that smashed into the north and east coasts of Crete. Some historians now believe that this brought the great Minoan civilization to a dramatic end.

▼ A telephone box is buried in mud, along with the rest of the town of Plymouth, on the Caribbean island of Montserrat after the 1997 eruption of Mount Soufriere. The intense sunset, caused by the scattering of volcanic dust, is called a volcanic twilight.

Sleeping giants

There are at least 500 active volcanoes across the planet that erupt regularly. Every year an average of about 50 actually erupt. Fortunately, most happen in places where few or no people live, such as the ocean floor, and, as a result, many go unnoticed. However, a few bring disaster. The highest death tolls tend to occur in less developed countries, where there are no volcano warning systems and communications are basic.

▲ This spectacular aerial view shows a hot spring in Yellowstone National Park, USA. It is heated by underground volcanic activity and is just one indication of a supervolcano below the surface.

◄ In 1994, scientists sent this robot into the crater of Mount Spurr, Alaska, USA. It was designed to study the interior of this active volcano, and take gas samples and video images.

Studying volcanoes

Although we have sent spacecraft millions of kilometres into space, it is much more difficult to explore more than a few kilometres below the earth's surface. Because of the high temperatures, the current limit for drills and other testing equipment is about 9km. Magma and other volcanic materials come from far deeper than this. Volcanologists – the scientists who study volcanoes – do most of their work on the surface, observing lava flows and pyroclastic outbursts.

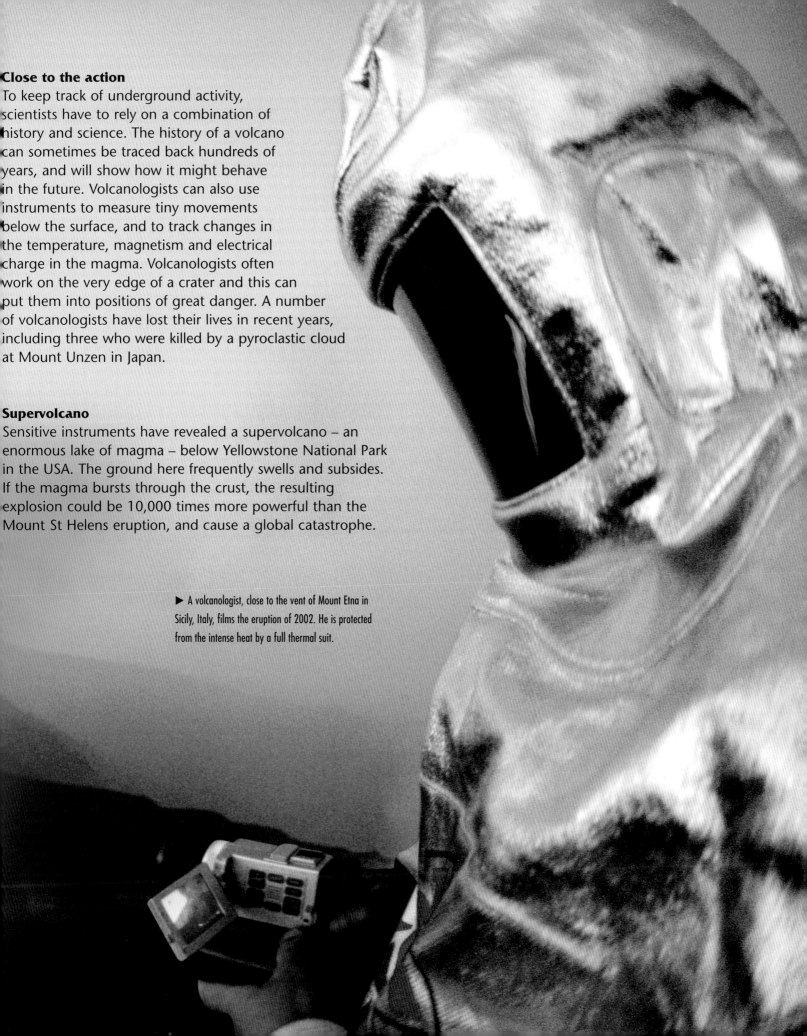

Close to the action

To keep track of underground activity, scientists have to rely on a combination of history and science. The history of a volcano can sometimes be traced back hundreds of years, and will show how it might behave in the future. Volcanologists can also use instruments to measure tiny movements below the surface, and to track changes in the temperature, magnetism and electrical charge in the magma. Volcanologists often work on the very edge of a crater and this can put them into positions of great danger. A number of volcanologists have lost their lives in recent years, including three who were killed by a pyroclastic cloud at Mount Unzen in Japan.

Supervolcano

Sensitive instruments have revealed a supervolcano – an enormous lake of magma – below Yellowstone National Park in the USA. The ground here frequently swells and subsides. If the magma bursts through the crust, the resulting explosion could be 10,000 times more powerful than the Mount St Helens eruption, and cause a global catastrophe.

▶ A volcanologist, close to the vent of Mount Etna in Sicily, Italy, films the eruption of 2002. He is protected from the intense heat by a full thermal suit.

SUMMARY OF CHAPTER 2: VOLCANOES

Erupting lava

Volcanoes usually occur at the edges of tectonic plates. Some volcanoes, however, are found at hot spots, which are located in the middle of the earth's plates. During a volcanic eruption, molten rock, called magma, forces its way up from deep below the surface. The magma, mixed with gases, pushes through a vent, or opening, and flows out as lava. Ash, steam and gas clouds may erupt with it. The lava eventually cools and solidifies as rock. Solidified lava can take on different appearances depending on the temperature of the lava when it left the volcano.

Explosive volcanoes

If a volcano's vent becomes blocked by lava, there can be a build-up of gas and intense heat. This can result in a violent explosion of molten rock, ash and hot gas. This kind of eruption is called a pyroclastic flow, and can cause complete devastation in the vicinity. Volcanic eruptions can also have a huge impact on places much further away. They can create tsunamis, which flood coasts thousands of kilometres away. The giant ash clouds blasted out during an eruption can reach high into the atmosphere and reduce the sun's heating effect on the earth. This can result in a lowering of global temperatures. The ash can also mix with water to form deadly mudflows.

A plaster cast of one of the victims of Mount Vesuvius, which erupted in 79CE burying Pompeii and Herculaneum in ash

Volcanologists at work

There are at least 500 volcanoes throughout the world that are active and might erupt. On average, about 50 of these erupt each year. Scientists, called volcanologists, perform vital work studying the behaviour of volcanoes. They take measurements, such as temperature below the surface, and monitor underground movements in order to keep track of active volcanoes. A volcano's history can also provide clues that help volcanologists predict eruptions.

Go further...

For tips about predicting eruptions, interactive games and video clips, visit: www.learner.org/exhibits/volcanoes

Discover more about active volcanoes around the world at: volcano.und.nodak.edu

Read about Jupiter's highly volcanic moon, Io, at: www.nineplanets.org/io.html

The Volcano Adventure Guide by Rosaly Lopes (Cambridge University Press, 2005)

Volcanoes: Fire from the Earth by Maurice Krafft (Thames & Hudson, 1993)

Astrogeologist
Studies surface conditions and features on moons and planets.

Geochemist
Specializes in the study of the earth's composition, analyzing rock, soil and gases.

Geomorphologist
Investigates the origin of landforms and the processes that shape them.

Igneous petrologist
Investigates how magma cools and forms different kinds of lava.

Volcanologist
Studies volcanoes and helps to predict volcanic eruptions.

See Mount St Helens, and, if the conditions are right, climb to the crater rim: Visitor Center, 3029 Spirit Lake Highway, Castle Rock, WA 98611, USA Telephone: +1 360 274 0962 www.fs.fed.us/gpnf/mshnvm/

Experience one of Europe's most active volcanoes, Mount Etna, in Sicily, Italy. You can arrange a guided tour and learn more about the volcano at the visitors' centre at: Via Etnea, 107/A, 95030 Nicolosi (CT), Sicily, Italy Telephone +1 39 95 914588

An approaching tornado in South Dakota, USA

CHAPTER 3

Storm, flood and snow

Earthquakes and volcanoes begin deep under the earth. Other natural hazards come from above the planet's surface in the form of weather. From a heavy snowfall that can start an avalanche to a ferocious hurricane hitting a coastal town, the world's weather is governed by three simple elements – water, air and heat. The heat of the sun evaporates water from the oceans, turning it into invisible water vapour. Warm air rises, so the water vapour is carried up into the sky.

Eventually, it reaches a colder region of air, where it turns into tiny droplets that form clouds. But just as warm air rises, cold air sinks. These forces moving in opposite directions produce winds and air currents. The winds together with the clouds produce all kinds of extreme weather across the world, including severe thunderstorms and tornadoes. Storms often bring heavy rainfall that can cause rivers to burst their banks, flooding vast areas of land.

Danger in the air

The atmosphere is a layer of air wrapped around our planet. It protects us from the sun's harmful radiation and helps to keep the earth warm. The atmosphere extends upwards from the surface for about 1,000km, but the world's weather takes place in the lowest and smallest part. This is called the troposphere, which reaches about 10km into the sky. Here, the air is always moving, carrying heat and moisture around the globe. Too much movement can generate giant storms that cause devastation in the form of tornadoes, hurricanes and floods.

▲ This satellite image shows the earth's cloud cover in three-dimensions. Many of these clouds will bring severe storms, accompanied by lightning, thunder, hail and heavy rain.

What is wind?

Wind is air that moves in a horizontal direction (air moving vertically is called a current). Winds are created by the uneven heating of the earth by the sun. Warm air rises and cold air rushes in to take its place. When this air blows across the land, features such as mountains, hills and woodlands often slow it down. These obstacles break up the wind into gusts and eddies, known as air turbulence. These do not often pose a great danger. When wind blows across the sea, however, it travels much faster, drawing up heat and moisture from the water.

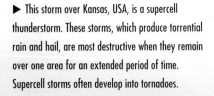

► This storm over Kansas, USA, is a supercell thunderstorm. These storms, which produce torrential rain and hail, are most destructive when they remain over one area for an extended period of time. Supercell storms often develop into tornadoes.

Storm birth

The weather acts as a kind of safety valve for the earth, preventing any one area of the world from getting too hot or too cold. It works by shifting hot air to cold places, and cold air to hot places. The warmest part of the world is the tropical region on either side of the Equator. This produces a vast amount of hot and moist air, which rises and then flows towards the North and South poles, where the air is coldest. This movement of air restores the balance of heat in the atmosphere, but it can also trigger storms by creating very strong winds and massive storm clouds that drop rain, hail or snow. Most storms begin life where the winds are strongest of all – over the ocean.

▲ Force 12 winds can overturn light aircraft and even toss them into trees. These two were destroyed by Hurricane Gilbert, which struck Kingston, Jamaica, in September 1988.

The Beaufort scale

In 1805, Francis Beaufort, a captain in the British Royal Navy, devised a system for judging the speed of the wind. A modified version is still used today, and is known as the Beaufort scale. At one end of the scale is Force 0 ('calm'), where there is almost no wind and smoke rises vertically. Halfway along the scale is Force 6 ('strong breeze'), where winds reach 50km/h, small trees sway, and telegraph wires whistle. Near gale, gale, strong gale and severe gale follow. When wind speeds hit 102km/h, Force 11 ('violent storm') has been reached. Trees may be flattened and cars overturned. Force 12 is in progress when the winds exceed 120km/h. This is classed as a hurricane – buildings are destroyed and there may be loss of life.

◄ Scientists from the Severe Thunderstorm Electrification and Precipitation Study (STEPS) get ready to launch a weather balloon into the storm cloud. The balloon carries instruments that record temperature, wind speed, air pressure and the electrical charges inside a storm.

Hurricane alert

Hurricanes are the planet's most ferocious storms. Known as cyclones in Australia and typhoons in southeast Asia, they bring with them massive waves and wind speeds that can gust up to 300km/h. Nearly all hurricanes are formed in the warm waters of the tropics. Each year, southeast and southern Asia are battered by over 30 hurricanes. The hurricane season also brings death and devastation to southern parts of the USA and Central America.

▶ Flying debris is a major hazard when a hurricane hits the coast. Hurricanes, which draw their energy from the sea, lose their power as they move inland.

Birth of a hurricane

A hurricane is made up of bands of thunderclouds spinning around a clear, still centre. Winds blowing across the warm seas near the Equator suck up heat and water vapour to form the storms that produce hurricanes. The swirling mass of thunderclouds is set spinning by the rotation of the earth and by winds from the poles. A hurricane can last for weeks and travel many thousands of kilometres.

▼ This satellite picture shows Hurricane Ivan over the Caribbean sea in September 2004. When it struck Grenada, over three-quarters of the island's homes were badly damaged.

Landfall

Over the ocean, hurricanes are a threat to ships, but when they reach land the dangers are much greater. The strength of the wind can tear down trees and flatten buildings. As well as whipping up massive waves, hurricanes can also cause a rise in the ocean level, or storm surge, which can drive the sea far inland.

Hurricane Katrina

Hurricane Katrina hit the USA on 29 August 2005. Winds of 225km/h created a 9m storm surge. Water breached the dykes that protected the city of New Orleans and flooded the low-lying coastlines of Louisiana, Alabama and Mississippi. With damage estimated at more than $200 million, and over a million people forced to leave their homes, Katrina is the costliest and most destructive natural disaster in US history.

▶ Hurricane Andrew, which struck Florida in August 1992, was one of the most powerful hurricanes of the last century. Over 100,000 homes were badly damaged and many residential areas, such as this trailer park, were flattened.

Twister

When a tornado descends from a storm cloud and touches down on land, it can leave a terrible trail of destruction in its wake. The Tri-State twister, which ripped through the US states of Missouri, Illinois and Indiana in 1925, demolished nine towns and killed almost 700 people. A tornado's path is almost impossible to predict. One house in a street might be flattened, while the neighbouring homes are left untouched. Twisters have also been known to suck up the water from rivers and even lift trains from their tracks.

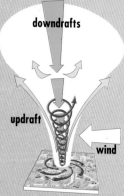

downdrafts

updraft

wind

▲ Tornadoes form when warm, rising air, called the updraft, is set spinning by winds blowing from the side.

Born from a storm
Tornadoes, like hurricanes, are violent winds that spiral around a still centre. They are formed during severe thunderstorms and are often accompanied by severe lightning and hail. Unlike a hurricane, a tornado's lifespan is much shorter – usually only a few minutes – and its base can be as narrow as 50m in diameter. The spinning winds, which cause most of the damage, can reach an incredible 500km/h.

◄ The furiously spinning winds of a tornado can carry cars and other objects through the air. Cattle and people have been lifted from the ground and dropped hundreds of metres away. Even weak twisters have enough power to rip roofs from houses and overturn cars.

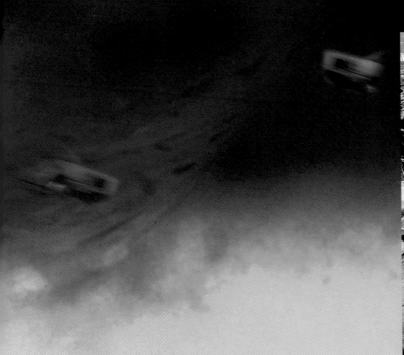

Under pressure

Tornado damage is also caused by differences in air pressure. This happens when the speed of the wind lowers the air pressure on the outside surface of a house. The air pressure inside stays the same, which means that it is higher than the outside, causing the house to explode. The roof lifts up and the side walls blow out. Engineers have not yet found a way of constructing a building that will stand up to this sort of treatment.

▲ Tornadoes are common in Bangladesh where powerful thunderstorms develop at the beginning of the monsoon season in April and May. In 1989, a tornado killed an estimated 1,300 people. The loss of life is often high because buildings are poorly constructed and the region is densely populated.

Across the world

There are about 1,000 tornadoes each year in the USA. Most occur in the area known as Tornado Alley, which includes the states of Nebraska, Kansas, Oklahoma and Texas. Here, warm, moist air from the Gulf of Mexico meets cold, dry air from the Rockies, creating ideal conditions for the formation of twisters. Less violent tornadoes, however, also happen in many other countries including Bangladesh, South Africa, Japan and the United Kingdom.

▲ This distinctive cloud formation, called 'mammatus', hangs from the underside of a storm cloud in Alberta, Canada. It is often a sign that a very severe thunderstorm or tornado is on its way.

Danger at sea

▲ A waterspout is a tornado that forms over water. Although rarer and less violent than twisters, waterspouts can pose a danger to shipping.

More than 200 super-tankers and giant container vessels have sunk because of severe weather in the last 20 years. Rogue, or freak, waves, which can reach heights of 30m (as high as a 12-storey building), were probably responsible for many of the losses. Although rogue waves are rare, plenty of people have experienced these terrifying monsters. In 1995, an offshore oil platform in the North Sea was hit by a wave measuring 26m high. The cruise liner *Queen Elizabeth II* survived one just as big a month later and other ships have been damaged by even higher waves.

Freak waves

Rogue waves were once believed to be the stuff of legend. However, recent studies, using data from satellites and radar, have proved their existence beyond doubt. At one site in the North Sea, 466 rogue waves were recorded over a period of 12 years. In 2000, the European Union set up a project called MaxWave to monitor the seas and learn more about these waves. The findings of this project are now being used to improve the design of ships.

◄ One of the most famous prints by the Japanese artist Hokusai, from about 1830, shows a huge wave threatening some boats below. Mount Fuji can be seen in the background. During severe storms, waves, whipped up by the wind, can reach heights of 15m or more.

◀ A giant wave smashes into the lighthouse outside a harbour on France's Atlantic coast in November 2000. The storm was so severe that a round-the-world yacht race was postponed for three days.

Waterspouts

Waterspouts are spinning funnels of air that can draw up water from a lake or sea to heights of up to 900m. Unlike tornadoes they do not need a storm cloud in order to form. Waterspouts rarely last longer than 15 minutes. Most waterspouts occur in the warm waters of the tropics but they have also been known to form in cooler climates. In December 1879, three waterspouts slammed into the Tay bridge in Scotland. The bridge was already weakened by gales, and the waterspouts caused a large section to collapse, just as a train was crossing. The train plunged into the river below, killing 75 people.

Unstable waves

Some scientists believe that rogue waves, which occur far out at sea, form when two strong currents meet. The currents push together, building up waves that are much higher than normal. It has also been suggested that some storm waves can become unstable when they are moving at high speed. When this happens, the unstable wave sucks in energy from other local waves and may increase in size very quickly. Some of these giant waves have been known to come in groups of three.

▼ This print shows rescue boats searching for bodies among wreckage from the train that fell into the River Tay, Scotland, when a bridge collapsed after it was hit by a cluster of waterspouts.

▼ A fishing boat is dwarfed by a giant wave in a scene from the film *The Perfect Storm* (2000). The title refers to the ideal conditions that came together to create a fierce storm that hit the east coast of North America in 1991.

Floods

Floods are the most deadly of all natural disasters. They have been a feature of many myths and religious writings since recorded history began. Nearly half of all disaster victims die from drowning or from the effects of flooding, such as starvation (when crops are ruined) and diseases, such as dysentery and typhoid, which thrive in water. There are many natural causes of flooding, including hurricanes, torrential rains and tsunamis. Unfortunately, many people live in places which are at risk of being flooded. About half of the world's population have their homes near rivers, or on low coastal land.

▲ When the Yangtze river overflowed in August 1998, the Chinese government evacuated hundreds of thousands of people. A third of China's 1.2 billion people live in the Yangtze river valley.

Bangladesh disaster

Bangladesh suffers the misery of floods from two directions. Melt water roars down the great rivers from the Himalayan mountains, while hurricanes (known as cyclones in this region) cause storm surges that overrun the low-lying shores. The tragic pattern has been repeated many times. Catastrophic floods killed two million people in 1970. The storms of 1998 brought more misery and made millions homeless.

China's Sorrow

China, too, experiences flooding on a huge scale. The Yangtze river, known as 'China's Sorrow', carries a rich load of silt which creates very fertile land on the plains, and many farmers grow crops there. Over the centuries they have built up dykes to hold back the water during the wet season, but the river has frequently broken through. Over two million people perished in the floods of 1887.

▼ Torrential rainfall deluged western India in July 2005. The resulting floods devastated the city of Mumbai and affected 20 million people in the region. Here, people hold onto a rope as they cross a street submerged by the floodwater.

El Niño

South America

▲ This satellite image shows the current of warm water called *El Niño*. Every five to seven years it heads towards South America, bringing heavy rainfall and flooding.

▲ In 1953, low-lying coastal areas of the Netherlands and eastern England were devastated by severe flooding.

At high risk

Some coastlines are sinking putting them at great risk from flooding. This has been happening for centuries to parts of southeast England and the Netherlands. In January 1953, a storm roared down the east coast of England, building up a vast bank of water. The storm surge came at the same time as a very high tide, breaching the sea walls. Thousands of homes were destroyed and over 2,000 people were drowned in England and the Netherlands.

Avalanche

In May 1970, a powerful earthquake shook the Andes mountains in Peru. The ice cap from the summit of Peru's highest peak, Mount Huascaran, shattered, sending thousands of tonnes of rock smashing onto a glacier. An 80m high wall of snow, ice, rock and mud hurtled down the mountainside at more than 320km/h. Within four minutes, the avalanche had buried the ski resort of Yungay. At least 25,000 people died in this disaster.

▲ These rescue workers are training to locate avalanche victims, using long rods called probes. The huge weight of the snow makes it almost impossible for people caught in an avalanche to dig their way out.

Triggers

A build-up of snow on the upper slopes can become a lethal avalanche, especially if snow on the lower slopes becomes unstable because of heavy rain. Without proper support, a giant slab of snow and ice can break free and sweep down the mountainside. Avalanches can be set off by a variety of events, including a strong wind, a change in temperature, or a skier coming down a slope.

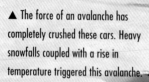

▲ The force of an avalanche has completely crushed these cars. Heavy snowfalls coupled with a rise in temperature triggered this avalanche.

An avalanche roars down a mountainside, collecting rocks and trees that add to its destructive power. An avalanche can also generate high-speed winds, called the sigh of the avalanche, that flatten trees and buildings.

Alpine disaster

Each year, about 100 people are killed by avalanches in the European Alps. The winter of 1998 to 1999 was particularly deadly, because of unusually heavy snowfall in the region. Some areas had up to six times more snow than average, creating ideal conditions for avalanches. On 24 February 1999, a vast slab of snow, 100m high and weighing over 200,000 tonnes, came away from a mountainside in Austria and smashed into the village of Galtür. In less than a minute, the village disappeared under an 8m thick blanket of snow, and 31 people lost their lives.

Avalanche survival

If you are caught in an avalanche you have only a one in twenty chance of survival. Many victims are killed by the sheer force of the falling snow or ice. If they survive this and are buried in the snow, they need to be rescued within 15 minutes. After this time, they will run out of air to breathe, and suffer from hypothermia (loss of body heat). Rescuers use heat detectors, sound detectors and radar to locate people trapped under snow, as well as the much more traditional method of specially trained dogs.

▼ Rescue workers sift through the area flooded by the overflow from the Vaiont dam, northern Italy, in October 1963, after a massive rockslide crashed into the lake. Nearly 2,000 people living in the valley were drowned. Before the dam was built, engineers had pointed out that there was a high risk of landslides in the region.

Fighting back

Meteorologists have a wide array of tools to make short-range and long-range weather forecasts, and to monitor the progress of extreme weather conditions. These include weather balloons, launched several times a day to measure wind and temperatures, and satellite images that reveal the tell-tale cloud spirals of a hurricane forming over the ocean. Such information can be used to alert people to severe weather well in advance so that they can take necessary action.

Tracking storms

Radar has proved one of the most effective instruments in forecasting. Weather-radar networks scan the skies, sending out pulses of radio waves. These bounce back when they meet a target, such as raindrops, snow or hail, enabling meteorologists to build up a detailed picture of weather systems. Doppler radar, which measures changes in the returning echoes, can even help to predict the formation of tornadoes.

▲ In this experiment, lightning in a thundercloud is artificially triggered by a rocket. Attached to the rocket is a copper wire, which provides a path for the lightning to reach instruments back on the surface. The experiment provides scientists with a better understanding of the processes that produce violent storms.

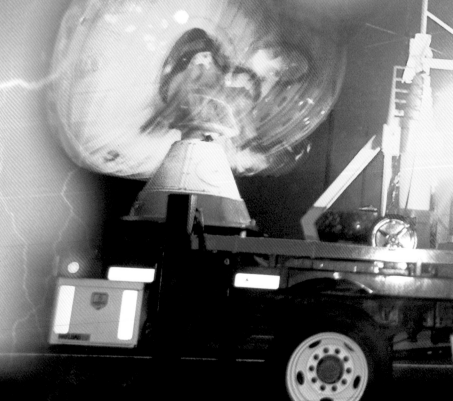

▶ This special truck is equipped with doppler radar, which can detect the direction and speed of a violent storm. It can help forecasters identify where hail, heavy rainfall and tornadoes are likely to form.

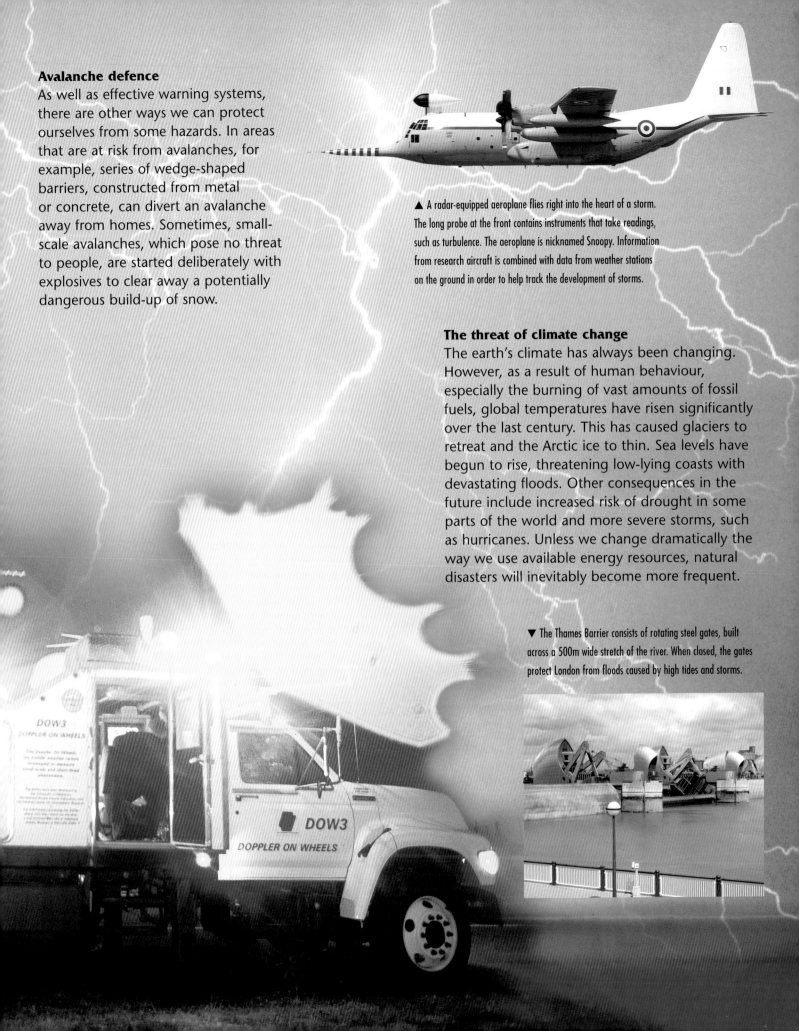

Avalanche defence

As well as effective warning systems, there are other ways we can protect ourselves from some hazards. In areas that are at risk from avalanches, for example, series of wedge-shaped barriers, constructed from metal or concrete, can divert an avalanche away from homes. Sometimes, small-scale avalanches, which pose no threat to people, are started deliberately with explosives to clear away a potentially dangerous build-up of snow.

▲ A radar-equipped aeroplane flies right into the heart of a storm. The long probe at the front contains instruments that take readings, such as turbulence. The aeroplane is nicknamed Snoopy. Information from research aircraft is combined with data from weather stations on the ground in order to help track the development of storms.

The threat of climate change

The earth's climate has always been changing. However, as a result of human behaviour, especially the burning of vast amounts of fossil fuels, global temperatures have risen significantly over the last century. This has caused glaciers to retreat and the Arctic ice to thin. Sea levels have begun to rise, threatening low-lying coasts with devastating floods. Other consequences in the future include increased risk of drought in some parts of the world and more severe storms, such as hurricanes. Unless we change dramatically the way we use available energy resources, natural disasters will inevitably become more frequent.

▼ The Thames Barrier consists of rotating steel gates, built across a 500m wide stretch of the river. When closed, the gates protect London from floods caused by high tides and storms.

SUMMARY OF CHAPTER 3: STORM, FLOOD AND SNOW

Winds

The world's weather occurs in the lowest part of the atmosphere, the blanket of air that surrounds and protects our planet. The sun's heat causes air to rise, and cold air rushes in to take its place. This movement of air produces wind and prevents any single area from getting too hot or too cold. On land, the wind is slowed down by hills, mountains and other features. Out at sea, however, there is nothing to break up the wind, and this is where most violent storms begin.

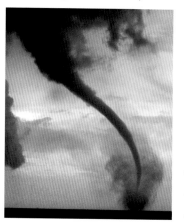

Hurricanes and tornadoes

A storm with winds of over 120km/h is classed as a hurricane. Hurricanes are formed when strong winds draw up heat and water

The rapidly rotating funnel of a waterspout, with spray at its base, near Cyprus in the eastern part of the Mediterranean sea

vapour from the warm seas near the Equator. This generates a mass of thunderclouds which is set spinning by the earth's rotation. When hurricanes make landfall, the violent winds often bring destruction over a wide area. Hurricanes can be accompanied by storm surges that sweep the sea inland, causing widespread flooding. Tornadoes are much smaller spinning storms, formed over land during severe thundestorms. Although most twisters last only a few minutes, their ferocious wind speeds of up to 500km/h can be deadly in populated areas.

The impact of floods

Floods kill more people than any other type of disaster. There are many natural causes of flooding, including storm surges created by hurricanes, torrential rains and tsunamis. Many people live in places that are at high risk of being flooded, such as low-lying coasts and river valleys, where the land is often very fertile and good for farming. Climate change, made worse by human activity, such as the burning of fossil fuels, has raised the level of the ocean and made floods even more likely in the future.

Go further...

Visit the official site of the US National Hurricane Center at:
www.nhc.noaa.gov

Explore every aspect of the weather and climate at:
www.metoffice.co.uk

Find out what storm chasers do and join them as they track wild weather at: www.stormchaser.com

Flood by Sean Connolly (Franklin Watts, 2004)

Eyewitness: Hurricane & Tornado by Jack Challoner (Dorling Kindersley, 2004)

Civil engineer
An engineer who designs and builds public structures, including dams and flood prevention schemes.

Climatologist
Specializes in the history of the planet's climate over hundreds or even millions of years.

Meteorologist
Studies the earth's atmosphere and makes predictions about the weather.

Storm chaser
Tracks down storms, including hurricanes and tornadoes to photograph or study them.

Visit the Thames Barrier at: The Thames Barrier Learning Centre, Unity Way, Woolwich, London SE18 5JN, UK
Telephone: +44 (0)20 8305 4188

See the Meteorology Gallery at: The Science Museum, Exhibition Road, South Kensington, London SW7 2DD, UK
Telephone: +44 (0)870 870 4868
www.sciencemuseum.org.uk

The Weather Gallery has a fantastic working model of twister at:
The National Center for Atmospheric Research (NCAR), 1850 Table Mesa Dr., Boulder, CO 80305, USA
Telephone +1 303 497 1174
www.eo.ucar.edu/visit

Chemicals that kill rats and cockroaches are sprayed in the Chinese city of Guangzhou to prevent the spread of disease

CHAPTER 4

Drought, fire and disease

Earthquakes, storms and many other natural hazards usually happen over a relatively short period of time. Even the most destructive hurricane loses its power after a few days. There are other natural disasters, however, that can last for years, and even decades. Their effects may be so devastating that full recovery is not possible. Drought, caused by lower-than-average rainfall, is a long-term threat in very arid places, bringing famine, poverty and illnesses related to malnutrition.

Where there is little water, there is also the danger of wildfire, started by lightning or by human action. These fires can spread with terrifying speed over vast areas, burning down forests and threatening urban areas. However, an invisible killer is perhaps the deadliest of all. Infectious diseases, such as smallpox and the plague, killed millions of people in the past. Other diseases, such as malaria, have brought sickness and death to some parts of the world for centuries.

▲ Villagers collect water from a well in Gujarat, India, during the severe drought that affected the region in 2003. During a drought, people often have to travel great distances in order to find supplies of clean drinking water.

▲ A giant dust cloud sweeps across homes in Texas, USA, in 1935. During the 1930s, drought turned farmland into a wasteland, known as the Dust Bowl, from Kansas to New Mexico.

Drought and famine

Humans cannot last long without water. Life-giving crops need it in order to grow. If there is not enough water, then plants, animals and people will die through dehydration or starvation. Large areas of the world suffer from drought which is caused mainly by a lack of rain. About one-third of the earth's land surface is classed as arid, which means it gets less than 25cm of rainfall in a year. The millions of people who live in these arid areas face starvation and death if the rains fail.

Famine in the Sahel

The southern edge of the Sahara desert, called the Sahel, stretches across eight countries in Africa, from Senegal to the Sudan. Since the 1960s, the annual rainfall in this desert region has been far below normal. The lack of water for irrigation results in the regular failure of crops. This has led to an almost permanent famine in some areas. In a prolonged drought between 1968 and 1973, as many as 250,000 people and 3.5 million cattle died. Starving families scoured the bare land in a desperate search for wild seeds and corn husks to eat. Since then, repeated droughts have created frequent famines, most recently in the south of Niger in 2005.

Increasing desert

Along the northern edge of the Sahara, about 1,000km^2 of land becomes desert every year. Below average rainfall is the main factor, but some scientists believe it is also caused by the growing population and the demand for food and living space. Grazing cattle and goats eat all the vegetation, and people cut down trees for firewood. This leaves the soil parched and bare, and it reverts to desert, unable to support people.

Tragedy in China

In poorer nations, drought has taken a terrible toll over the last century. Between 1965 and 1967, starvation caused by drought resulted in 1.5 million deaths in India, while in Ethiopia, in 1984 and 1985, over one million people lost their lives. The combination of drought and human behaviour can also have horrific consequences. During the 1950s, China's Communist leader, Mao Zedong, ordered millions of farmers to leave their homes and fields to work in factories. This resulted in massive food shortages. When a drought hit the country at the same time, it has been estimated that between 30 and 40 million people died in the resulting famine.

Wildfires

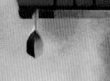

In hot, dry regions, where the sun parches the vegetation, wildfires can take hold with terrifying speed. Fuelled by strong winds, they race across vast distances in North America, parts of Australia and southern Europe, destroying buildings, trees and crops. Although wildfires can bring disaster to populated areas, not all their consequences are bad. They can clear away deadwood in forests, leave fertile ash in the soil and help to germinate the seeds of some trees.

▲ Flames and smoke from wildfires loom above the Simi valley, California, USA, in October 2003. Fierce, dry winds drove the fires over a wide area, burning many hundreds of homes.

▲ Lightning is the most common cause of wildfire. When lighting strikes the ground, it can heat soil to temperatures of up to 1,800°C and instantly set alight vegetation. Some wildfires are started deliberately by people, or caused by carelessness, such as campfires that have not been extinguished.

Bushfires

In summer, searing temperatures and drought provide the ideal conditions for outbreaks of bushfires in parts of Australia, including New South Wales and Victoria. Forests of eucalyptus trees are also found here – their oily bark and leaves are set alight very easily and burn fiercely. Strong winds can blow flaming scraps of bark over 30km, starting dozens of new fires. During bushfires in the Blue mountains, in 2001, firefighters struggled to cope with hundreds of scattered blazes. The fire burned an area twice the size of London, and threatened the suburbs of Sydney. Even more disastrous fires in 1983 resulted in the deaths of 72 people.

◄ This specially adapted aeroplane scoops up water as it flies across a lake and drops it onto fires. Air tankers of this type can also spray chemicals that slow down and cool the flames.

Fighting fire

In areas that are at risk from wildfire, surveillance aircraft make regular patrols in summer and autumn, looking for small fires and observing how they spread. On the ground, fire crews may dig trenches called firebreaks to create gaps in the vegetation, and try to douse the flames with water, flame-retarding chemicals or sand. Aeroplanes can also spray fire retardants and water in an attempt to minimize the fire spreading. Sometimes, however, only heavy rainfall can quench the flames.

Scorched earth

Wildfires can spread at speeds of up 23km/h – faster than a person can run. Most burn themselves out quickly, but some can last for weeks raging across the landscape. The most deadly recorded wildfire broke out near Peshtigo, Wisconsin, USA, in October 1871. It raced over 6,000km^2 of parched grass and woodland, killing 1,500 people on the way. The most costly wildfire hit Oakland, California, USA, in 1991, destroying homes and causing $1.5 billion worth of damage.

▼ Firefighters on the ground wear protective clothing against the intense heat of the fire.

Invisible killers

Some of the deadliest natural killers in the world are so tiny that you can see them only through the lens of a microscope. These lethal micro-organisms are the bacteria and viruses that spread infectious diseases. They are helped by an army of insects, worms and other creatures which carry infections from one person to another. Infectious disease kills millions of people every year across the planet.

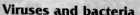

▲ The bilharzia flatworm begins life inside water snails, and penetrates the skin of humans and other animals. It travels in the blood to the liver and the intestines, causing illness and, frequently, death.

Viruses and bacteria

A virus is a simple package of chemicals. But once it gets inside a living cell, it can multiply very quickly, damaging the cell and eventually destroying it. Viruses are the cause of many common illnesses, including measles and chickenpox, as well as life-threatening ones, such as polio and SARS. Bacteria are also simple organisms. The vast majority are harmless, but some produce deadly diseases, such as cholera, which can spread rapidly.

▶ A mosquito pierces a person's skin with its proboscis, or mouthparts, to feed on blood. In this way, it can transmit a parasite called *Plasmodium*, which is responsible for malaria. The parasites multiply inside the host's red blood cells, before bursting out and infecting more blood cells. Mosquitoes can also pass on viral diseases such as dengue or yellow fever.

◀ The West Nile virus causes a disease called encephalitis, which inflames the brain. It is transmitted to people and animals by mosquitoes. In 2003, an outbreak of the virus in the USA resulted in over 250 human deaths.

Malaria

The biggest killer of all is malaria. This is carried by a type of mosquito, which passes on the infection when it bites a human and injects the disease into the bloodstream. Victims suffer from fever and cold, and may then fall into a coma and die. Every year, at least 200 million people are affected by malaria, which is very difficult to treat or cure. About two million of them die. Most victims are children living in the tropical and sub-tropical regions of the world, including Central Africa and South America.

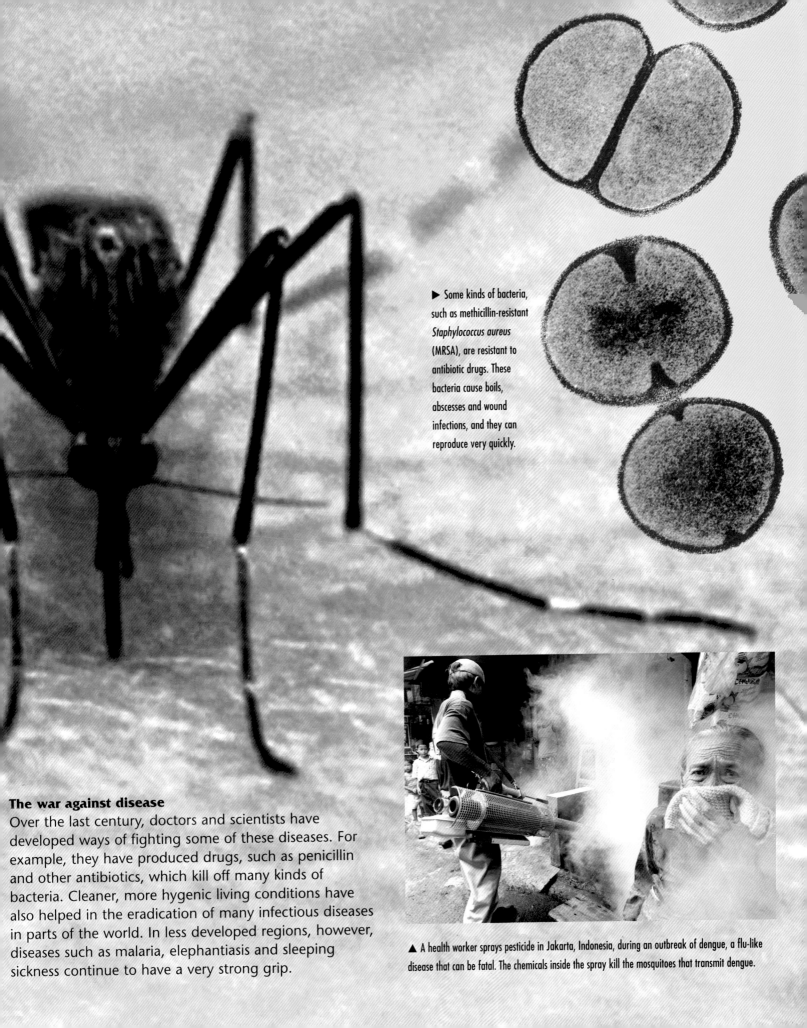

▶ Some kinds of bacteria, such as methicillin-resistant *Staphylococcus aureus* (MRSA), are resistant to antibiotic drugs. These bacteria cause boils, abscesses and wound infections, and they can reproduce very quickly.

The war against disease

Over the last century, doctors and scientists have developed ways of fighting some of these diseases. For example, they have produced drugs, such as penicillin and other antibiotics, which kill off many kinds of bacteria. Cleaner, more hygenic living conditions have also helped in the eradication of many infectious diseases in parts of the world. In less developed regions, however, diseases such as malaria, elephantiasis and sleeping sickness continue to have a very strong grip.

▲ A health worker sprays pesticide in Jakarta, Indonesia, during an outbreak of dengue, a flu-like disease that can be fatal. The chemicals inside the spray kill the mosquitoes that transmit dengue.

Pandemic

In October 1347, a fleet of ships arrived at Messina in Sicily, Italy. On board, everyone was dying, or already dead. Dark blotches covered the victims' skin, their bodies were swollen and their tongues were black. Although the sick were prevented from leaving the ships, no one could stop the rats, infested with fleas that carried the mystery infection, from scurrying ashore. Soon, the people of Messina had the same symptoms as the infected sailors.

▲ The rat flea *Xenopsylla cheopis* carries the bacterium that causes bubonic plague. The fleas feed off the blood of brown rats and other rats that live near humans in towns and villages.

▼ The black rat, or ship's rat, was the major carrier of the plague flea during the Black Death. Careful control of rats and fleas has rid much of Europe from plague, though it persists in some other parts of the world.

The Black Death
This was the beginning of the Black Death, one of the first great pandemics, or worldwide epidemics. The disease had been carried along trade routes from China through Russia and the Middle East, and then across the Mediterranean. From Messina, it spread rapidly through Italy, then raced across Germany, Spain and France, reaching England in the summer of 1348. Within four years, 23 million people had died – about one-third of Europe's population.

▶ This carved wooden mask was placed as a marker above a burial site for victims of the Black Death in Rouen, France.

A package of diseases
The Black Death consisted of three diseases, caused by a bacterium called *Yersina pestis*. The bubonic plague, which killed up to 75 per cent of its victims, and septicaemic plague, which killed over 90 per cent, were transmitted by fleas. Anyone who caught pneumonic plague was almost certain to die. Pneumonic plague was spread in droplets of saliva when individuals carrying the bacteria coughed and infected other people.

▶ Victims of the 1918 influenza epidemic lie in an army camp hospital in France. The pandemic occurred because a new kind of viral infection appeared. Humans had no immunity against this infection, so it spread very quickly, affecting at least one-fifth of the world's population.

Return of the plague

The Black Death faded away in 1351, but other plague epidemics have broken out over the centuries. In 1665, plague killed 100,000 people in London. In 1894, there was a major outbreak in China which spread as far as India and the USA, killing at least 10 million people in total. Despite modern medicines, up to 3,000 cases of plague are still recorded each year across the world.

▼ This woodcut represents the coming of the plague to Europe in the 1660s. To the right of the picture is a doctor wearing a beak mask. The beak was filled with strongly scented herbs.

A modern pandemic

One of the most deadly pandemics in history began at the end of the First World War in 1918 when a new and deadly strain of influenza appeared. Unlike more common influenzas, which usually strike the elderly and newborn, the 1918 Flu Epidemic targeted the young and healthy, as well as more vulnerable people. Passed from person to person, it swept across the world, and between 25 and 50 million people died.

Defending ourselves

In the war against natural hazards, humans do not have the upper hand. There is nothing we can do to prevent hurricanes, drought or new diseases from developing. However, we are not completely defenceless. Further research into understanding the causes of these hazards, backed up by the use of technology, will continue to make the difference between life and death.

▼ Irrigation systems that channel water to fields allow fertile land to flourish even in arid conditions.

Dealing with drought

Scientists now believe that there is a strong link between changes in sea surface temperatures and the periods of low rainfall that result in drought. More research needs to be done, but, in the future, accurate drought predictions might be reality. At a local level, measures such as effective crop selection and systems to conserve water are used in drought-prone areas. For example, earth structures, called bunds, stop rainwater from being washed away. Irrigation channels dug into the top of the bunds can also be used to bring water to crops.

▼ Schoolgirls in Peru wait in line to wash their hands at a new water tap. Almost three-quarters of the world's rural population have no access to clean and fresh water supplies. In many places, the water is contaminated with toxic chemicals or sewage.

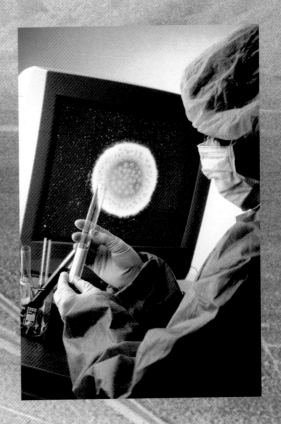

▶ Research by microbiologists is providing us with a much better understanding of how to combat infectious diseases. The screen shows an enlarged image of the virus that causes Lassa fever, a disease found in Africa and transmitted by rats.

The fight against disease

The most effective way to fight disease is to prevent it taking hold in the first place. The provision of clean drinking water and efficient sewerage (waste water) systems stop germs from breeding and spreading easily. The next crucial step is to make people immune to the diseases. This is done by giving them a vaccine – a mild form of the illness – that will stimulate the body into defending itself against the disease. Vaccination completely eradicated smallpox after a worldwide campaign during the 1970s.

The planet's most valuable resource

Over one billion people – one in six of the world's population – do not have access to clean drinking water. Almost 6,000 children die every day from diseases associated with unsafe water and poor hygiene. Technology can make a real difference, however. These include filter systems that remove the particles and microbes associated with illnesses such as diarrhoea, and solar disinfection which uses the sun's heat and radiation to make contaminated water clean enough to drink. Until recently, people in remote villages in Bangladesh often had to walk for hours in the searing heat to find supplies of water. Now, water is piped directly from the hills to many villages by gravity-flow systems. This allows people to draw clean, safe water at any time.

▶ A child in India is given a polio vaccine by mouth. Polio, which can cause paralysis, can be prevented by giving children the vaccine, which makes them immune to the virus. Vaccination programmes have reduced the number of people infected with the virus from hundreds of thousands each year to about a thousand.

SUMMARY OF CHAPTER 4: DROUGHT, FIRE AND DISEASE

Drought

Humans depend on water for survival. We need to drink it to stay alive and it supports the crops that give us food. Many parts of the world, however, suffer from drought, which occurs when there is insufficient rainfall. If the crops fail and livestock perish, drought can also lead to famine. About one third of the earth's land surface is arid. Famine is a long-term threat in many arid places, especially for the African countries that lie on the Sahel, the southern edge of the Sahara desert. Some of the world's deserts, including the Sahara, are increasing in size.

Lightning strikes

Hot, dry regions are at risk from wildfire. Very warm climates create parched vegetation and

Lightning strikes a tree during a powerful storm. If the vegetation is very dry and there are stong winds, a wildfire may start.

strong winds, as well as drying up water sources. In these conditions, lightning, as well as human carelessness, can easily start a fire that will spread very quickly. Firefighters deal with these blazes in a number of ways. These include building firebreaks and using flame-retarding chemicals. Once a wildfire takes hold, however, it can be very difficult to put out. Although wildfires bring great danger, especially in populated areas, they can benefit forests by clearing dead trees and leaving fertile ash in the soil.

Infectious diseases

Infectious diseases caused by bacteria and viruses are responsible for millions of deaths each year. The infections are often carried by hosts – other animals, including worms, snails and insects – which pass them on to humans. An epidemic is caused when an infectious disease spreads quickly among many people. If the disease spreads across the world it is called a pandemic. The provision of clean water and better living conditions, together with vaccinations and drugs such as penicillin, have helped combat diseases in many parts of the world.

Go further...

Learn more about wildfire and see firefighters in action at: http://www.nifc.gov

Find out how Australians deal with drought at: www.bom.gov.au/climate/drought/livedrought.shtml

For information on infectious diseases, go to the World Health Organization site at: www.who.int/topics/infectious_diseases

Fire and Drought
(A & C Black, 2006)

Fire in their Eyes: Wildfires and the People who Fight Them by Karen Magnuson Beil (Harcourt, 1999)

Agronomist
Researches ways to improve crops and the quality of seed.

Epidemiologist
Studies diseases and how they spread through populations.

Forest fire inspector
Monitors outbreaks of fire in national parks and forests.

Hydrologist
Researches the quantity and distribution of underground and surface water.

Virologist
Studies viruses and the diseases that they cause.

Visit the laboratory where penicillin was discovered: Alexander Fleming Laboratory Museum, St Mary's Hospital, Praed Street, London W2 1NY, UK
Telephone: +44 (0)20 78866528
www.st-marys.nhs.uk/about/fleming_museum.htm

See how the plague devastated London during the 1300s at the Medieval London gallery: The Museum of London, London Wall, London EC2Y 5HN, UK
Telephone:+44 (0)870 444 3852
www.museumoflondon.org.uk

Glossary

active volcano
A volcano that is erupting or is likely to do so in the future.

air pressure
The weight of the atmosphere as it presses on the surface of the earth.

antibiotic
A drug, such as penicillin, designed to treat bacterial infections.

ash
Very fine rock and mineral fragments created during a volcanic eruption.

asthenosphere
The semi-liquid layer of molten rock that lies beneath the lithosphere.

atmosphere
The blanket of gases (mainly oxygen, hydrogen and nitrogen) that forms an envelope around the earth, keeping it warm and protecting the planet from the sun's radiation.

bacteria
Microscopic organisms, some of which can cause diseases.

bubonic plague
An infectious and usually deadly epidemic disease transmitted by fleas.

core
The inner part of the planet, consisting of a solid central core and a molten outer core.

crater
A bowl-shaped hollow, often formed at the top of a volcano.

crust
The skin of rock that covers the surface of the earth.

cyclone
The name given to a hurricane in the Indian ocean and western Pacific.

desert
An area, either hot or cold, where the annual rainfall is less than 25cm.

drought
Prolonged shortage of water, caused when less rain than normal falls.

Rescue dog searching for earthquake survivors

dyke
An embankment, often made of earth, to prevent flooding.

epicentre
The point on the earth's surface directly above an earthquake's source.

epidemic
An outbreak of an infectious disease that affects a large number of people at the same time.

famine
A severe shortage of food, often caused by drought.

fault
A fracture in the earth's crust where two plates move against each other.

flame retardant
A chemical or material that will not burn and is used by firefighters to control and slow down a blaze.

fossil fuels
Coal, oil and natural gas, formed millions of years ago by the decay and fossilization of organic matter.

glacier
A slow-moving river of ice made from compacted snow that flows down a valley under its own weight.

hypothermia
Dangerously low body temperature caused by exposure to cold and wind.

intestine
The long tube that forms the lower part of a person's digestive system.

irrigation
The supply of water to fields by means of pipes, streams or channels dug in the ground.

lahar
Volcanic mudflow, often triggered by rapidly melting snow and ice following a volcanic eruption.

lava
The word for magma after it has reached the earth's surface.

lithosphere
The surface, or outer layer of the earth, that includes the crust and the upper part of the mantle.

magma
Molten rock formed under the earth's surface, just beneath the lithosphere.

magma chamber
An underground reservoir containing magma that feeds a volcano above.

magnitude
A measurement of the amount of energy released in an earthquake.

mantle
The thick layer of dense rocks that makes up most of the planet and lies below the crust and above the core.

meteorologist
Scientist who studies the weather.

pandemic
An epidemic that affects large numbers of people across the world.

parasite
An organism that grows and feeds on another kind of organism (such as an animal), but which does not do anything to benefit the host.

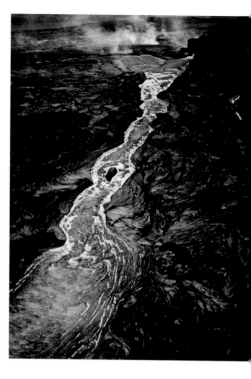

Lava flow from Kilauea, Hawaii, USA

plate tectonics
The theory that the earth's surface is divided into a number of moving plates, causing continents to shift, new ocean crust to form, and triggering volcanoes and earthquakes.

pneumonic plague
Infectious and deadly epidemic disease marked by inflammation and blockage of the lungs.

Primary Wave
A seismic wave that can travel through solid rock in the earth.

pyroclastic flow
Cloud made up of fragments of molten rock, ash and volcanic gas, which is ejected from a volcano during an explosive eruption.

Cast of a human body found at Pompeii, Italy

radar
A system used for detecting and locating distant objects, such as clouds, that works by measuring the time it takes for radio waves to be reflected back from the target.

reservoir
A body of water collected in an artificial or natural lake.

Ring of Fire
The region around the Pacific ocean, where the Pacific plate meets other plates, and where most of the planet's volcanoes and earthquakes occur.

rupture
A break or tear in the earth's surface.

seismic wave
A wave that runs through the earth, usually caused by an earthquake.

seismograph
An instrument for detecting and recording the strength and direction of seismic waves.

septicaemic plague
An infectious and deadly epidemic disease in which micro-organisms attack the blood system.

shield volcano
A gently sloping volcano, formed from fast-flowing lava.

storm surge
A rise in sea level that can cause severe flooding in coastal areas.

tremor
A shaking or vibrating movement in the earth's surface.

tropics
The warm regions to the north and south of the Equator.

troposphere
The lowest part of the atmosphere, directly above earth's surface.

tsunamis
Waves, or series of waves, generated by a massive displacement of water, caused by earthquakes or explosive volcanic eruptions on the coast.

turbulence
Air that has become very agitated.

updraft
A movement of air away from the ground, typically found inside thunderstorms and tornadoes.

vaccination
A medicine, often given by injection, that protects against a disease.

vent
An opening inside the earth's crust that allows volcanic gases and molten rock to escape.

virus
A tiny chemical package that invades living cells and causes disease.

water vapour
Water in the form of gas.

Flyover destroyed by an earthquake in Kobe, Japan

waterspout
A spinning column of wind that sucks water up from lakes and seas.

weather balloon
A balloon used to carry meteorological instruments.

Index

Acknowledgements

The publisher would like to thank the following for permission to reproduce their material. Every care has been taken to trace copyright holders. However, if there have been unintentional omissions or failure to trace copyright holders, we apologize and will, if informed, endeavour to make corrections in any future edition.

Key: *b* = bottom, *c* = centre, *l* = left, *r* = right, *t* = top

Cover *left* Getty/Paula Bronstein; Cover *centre* Corbis/Raymond Gehman; Cover *centre background* Corbis/Stephen Dol; Cover *right* Corbis/Reuters; Cover *bottom* Getty Stone; page 1 Empics/AP; 2*l* Corbis/ Reuters; 2–3 Getty/NGS; 4–5 Corbis/Reuters; 7 Corbis/Charles O'Rear; 8*tl* Corbis/Reuters; 8–9 Corbis/Reuters; 9*tr* Science Photo Library (SPL); 10*tl* SPL/David Parker; 10*b* Getty/Hulton; 11*b* Corbis/Grant Smith; 11*tr* Getty/Koichi Kamoshida; 12*bl* Getty/Photonica; 13*tl* Getty/Time Life Pictures; 13*bl* Getty/AFP Bay Ismoyo; 14*tr* Science & Society Picture Library; 14*tl* Getty/AFP; 14*b* Getty/Spencer Platt; 15*b* Corbis/Punit Paranjpe Reuters; 15*tr* Getty/AFP Sena Vidanagama; 16*tl* Science & Society Picture Library; 16*bl* Corbis/Reuters; 17*bl* Popperfoto/Reuters; 17*tr* SPL/British Antarctic Survey; 19 Getty/NGS; 20*tl* SPL/Mark Garlick; 20*bl* SPL/Gary Hincks; 20–21 Getty; 21*br* SPL Christian Darkin; 21*tr* Corbis/Pierre Vauthey; 22*bl* Art Archive; 22*br(b)* SPL/Stephen & Donna O' Meara; 22*br(c)* SPL/G Brad Lewis; 22*br(t)* SPL/G Brad Lewis; 23*br* Planet Earth; 23*t* Getty/Imagebank; 24*tl(t)* Corbis; 24*tl(b)* Corbis; 24*bl* Corbis/Roger Ressmeyer; 24*cr* Frank Spooner Pictures/NASA/Liaison/B Ingalls; 25 Corbis; 26*tl* Getty Hulton; 26*bl* SPL/Robert M. Carey NOAA; 27*br* Panos Pictures; 28*bl* SPL NASA; 28*tr* Corbis Yann Arthus–Bertrand; 28–29 Getty NGS; 30 Art Archive; 31 Getty NGS; 32*cl* SPL/R B Huser NASA; 32–33 SPL/Jim Reed; 32*tr* SPL/John Beatty; 33*b* SPL Jim Reed; 33*tr* Sygma/ Bleibtreu/John Hillelson agency; 34*bl* SPL/NOAA; 34–35 Getty/Photonica; 35*br* Corbis/Roger Bell; 36–37 Photolibrary.com; 37*bl* Photolibarry.com; 37*tr* Getty/AFP Farjana Godhuly; 38*tl* Corbis/Reuters; 38*b* Corbis Historical Picture Archive; 39*tl* Corbis Reuters; 39*cr* Getty/Hulton; 39*b* Corbis Sygma; 40*tr* Empics 40–41 Empics; 41*tl* SPL NASA; 41*tr* Corbis Bettmann; 42*tl* Corbis Reuters; 42*bl* Rex Features; 42–43*t* SPL/W Bacon; 42–43*b* Zefa; 43*bl* Corbis David Lees; 44*cl* SPL Peter Menzel; 44–45*b* Getty NGS; 45*br* Rex Features; 46*tl* Corbis/Reuters; 47*t* Corbis China Photo Reuters; 48*bl* NOAA; 48–49 Still Pictures/Hartmut Schwarzbach; 50*tr* Getty/David Hume–Kennerly; 50*cl* Getty/Stone; 50–51 Getty/Stone; 51*b* Getty/David McNew; 51*t* Getty/David McNew; 52*tl* SPL/Russell Kightley; 52*cl* SPL Eye of Science; 52–53 Corbis/Timothy Fadek; 53*br* Corbis/Dadang Tri/Reuters; 53*tr* SPL/Biomedical Imaging Unit Southampton General Hospital; 54*tl* SPL/John Burbidge; 54*bl* Frank Lane Picture Agency/Foto Natura; 54–55*c* Corbis/Nicole Duplaix; 55*bl* Mary Evans Picture Library; 55*br* SPL; 55*tr* SPL/US Library of Medicine; 56*b* Corbis/Caroline Penn; 56–57 Getty/NGS; 57*br* SPL/S Nagendra; 57*tr* SPL Laurent/Bsip; 58*cl* Getty/Stone; 59*b* Corbis/Owen Franken; 60*tr* Getty/Taxi; 60*bl* Corbis/Roger Ressmeyer; 61*tr* Corbis/Reuters; 64 Corbis/Reuters

The publisher would like to thank the following illustrators: Sebastien Quigley (Linden Artists) (12–13, 32–33, 34–35, 42–43, 50–51); Peter Clayman (36–37)

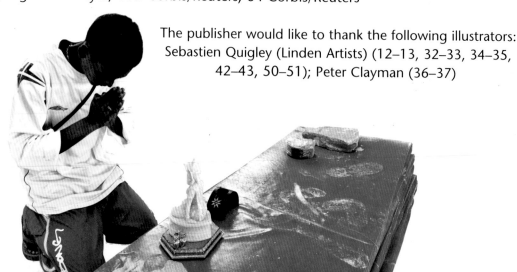